ALL
Orig

CAUTION: Pro⌐
that this play is subject t
Works Publishing, and the copyright laws of the United States. All rights, including professional, amateur, motion pictures, recitation, lecturing, public reading, radio broadcasting, television, and the rights of translation into foreign languages are strictly reserved.

The performance rights to this play are controlled by Original Works Publishing and royalty arrangements and licenses must be secured well in advance of presentation. PLEASE NOTE that amateur royalty fees are set upon application in accordance with your producing circumstances. When applying for a royalty quotation and license please give us the number of performances intended, dates of production, your seating capacity and admission fee. Royalties are payable with negotiation from Original Works Publishing.

Royalty of the required amount must be paid whether the play is presented for charity or gain and whether or not admission is charged. Particular emphasis is laid on the question of amateur or professional readings, permission and terms for which must be secured from Original Works Publishing through direct contact.

Copying from this book in whole or in part is strictly forbidden by law, and the right of performance is not transferable.

Whenever the play is produced the following notice must appear on all programs, printing, and advertising for the play:
"**Produced by special arrangement with
Original Works Publishing.
www.originalworksonline.com**"

Due authorship credit must be given on all programs, printing and advertising for the play.

Boy Small
© MT Cozzola
Trade Edition, 2016
ISBN 978-1-63092-086-9

Also Available From Original Works Publishing

Play Nice by Robin Rice

Synopsis: The Diamond siblings use the only resources they have, the dramatic role-play of their imaginations, to cope with the abusive Dragon Queen - their mother. Play Nice! is a mystery in which Isabel, Luce and Matilda embark on a journey within themselves to discover who poisoned her.

Cast Size: 3 Females, 1 Male

BOY SMALL
By MT Cozzola

Moral Clarity and Psychological Complexity: The World of "Boy Small"

By Michael F. Troy, Ph.D.,LP

"Who can understand such suffering as mine? I'd put money on it, not a soul." With his opening line, the title character in *Boy Small* captures the fundamental challenge to all who seek to understand the pathology of abuse.

As a clinical psychologist, my interest in this play was sparked by its dramatic exploration of that space within which parental commitment distorts into damaging control, and how a child's evolving sense of autonomy can lead to irresolvable conflict. Understanding the processes that drive typical child and adolescent development, as well as its deviations, has been the work of my career. *Boy Small* moved me, unsettled me, and caused me to see with a fresh perspective the human cost of adaptation to profoundly maladaptive circumstances.

The story of *Boy Small* is simple. Two adolescents strive to meet the challenges of growing up despite the fact that Boy lives in a dog cage and his sister is his keeper. Keeping a close watch are their frustrated father and his ambitious new wife. But Boy is bent on escape, no matter what the cost. The play was inspired by the heartbreaking story of an eleven-year-old Indiana child, Christian Choate, who died in 2011 as the result of abuse and neglect. The boy's father, Riley Choate, was convicted in 2013 for neglect and other crimes related to the case. At his sentencing he said, "All my actions will haunt me forever. I loved my son."

In the context of this fictional exploration of those events, Boy's fight to become his own person both sustains and ultimately destroys him. The paradox inherent in such a struggle is uniquely suited to a work of theatre, where it can be explored through multiple character perspectives and opposing objectives.

For professionals working with troubled families, Boy's fight resonates at several levels. It captures not only the brutality of abusive acts, but the brutality of fearing and anticipating such acts. It addresses with sophistication and sensitivity the larger web of intrapersonal and interpersonal issues that perpetuate abusive family systems. *Boy Small* also considers the well-intended, but often insufficient, community safeguards designed to protect and rescue maltreated children.

Of particular interest to students of social sciences is the play's dramatization of human development itself. In the character of Dad, we see how a parent's misinterpretation of normal-range developmental transitions cause him to see only attempts to undermine order and disrupt the status quo. Healthy development is a complex adaptive system, and watching the continual iterations of power and support in the relationship between Sissy and Boy reveals the unpredictability of that system. *Boy Small* shows how the natural developmental drives of each child can lead to distinct, dangerous trajectories.

Playwright MT Cozzola's grasp of developmental theory, both intuitive and informed, transforms *Boy Small* from a compelling story to a deeper and more meaningful exploration of how abuse and neglect can become embedded in family systems and maintained over time. She understands that ours is a social brain that develops within the context of relationships. It is seen in the universal drive to connect to others—a human drive that supersedes all others. Consequently, it is not a question of whether or not we form relationships, but rather the quality of the relationships—and how those relationships in turn affect who we become.

Perhaps most significantly, to me, is the way in which this play makes sophisticated developmental constructs accessible and relevant to a wide audience. *Environmental sensitivity*, for example, represents a domain of scientific inquiry rooted in developmental and evolutionary theory. At its heart, this approach suggests that children are, at a genetic and biological level, differentially susceptible to adverse conditions and responsive to supportive conditions. Some children, it is suggested, are markedly resilient in the face of stressful, challenging circumstances. These individuals are sometimes referred to as "dandelion children." Other children, known as "orchid children," seem to be especially reactive and damaged under such challenging circumstances. At the same time, however, growing up in an enriched environment may be of limited value for the dandelion child, while the orchid child flourishes under such conditions.

While the playwright may not have had this conceptual model specifically in mind, Sissy and Boy Small bring this theory to life in a compelling manner. While Sissy seems to weather the abusive and oppressive parenting of her father to some degree, she lacks both the spark and the vulnerability of her brother. Boy Small is unable to survive such a cruel and destructive home, but would surely have thrived had the conditions been right. He would have, we imagine, developed into an adult of erudition and insight. Indeed, he would have become someone like Boy Grown.

There are other, more general developmental principles clearly at work in this play as well. The concept of environmental sensitivity is a specific expression of the fact that human development is fundamentally contextual. In the context of the family represented in *Boy Small*, each child's adaptation to the father's pathology exacts a cost. Indeed, it is a reflection of Ms. Cozzola's psychological sophistication that she so clearly depicts both children in this story as victims–in one case immediate and obvious, and in the other insidious and indirect.

Boy Small, with its combination of moral clarity and psychological complexity, raises important questions for scholars, artists, and anyone seeking to foster a more healthy society. How is it that the role of parent can distort in form and function from protector to victimizer? What is the force that binds others to the victimizer and compels them to acquiesce and even enable acts of cruelty and abuse? Why does innocence and goodness seem to serve, by its very nature, as a provocation to evil? What sparks hope and empowers resistance in the face of seeming hopelessness?

There are no easy answers. But a work of art such as *Boy Small*, that examines without oversimplifying, helps to broaden and deepen our shared understanding of the challenges. Most importantly, it renews the vital resolve to never turn away from a child in need of rescue.

Michael F. Troy, Ph.D, LP
Medical Director, Behavioral Health Services
Associate Medical Director, Neuroscience Program
Children's Hospitals and Clinics of Minnesota

The world premiere of BOY SMALL was produced by The Fine Print Theatre in Chicago, Illinois, and opened on August 23, 2013. Jarrod Bainter designed the set and lighting, Ashley Ann Woods designed the costumes, Steve Labedz designed the sound, Mark E. Penzien was the fight choreographer, and Dave Belden composed the music. The assistant director was Emmi Hilger, and the stage manager was Sydney Ray.

The production was directed by Patrick Michael Kenney.

The cast was as follows:

BOY—Stephen Cefalu, Jr.

SISSY—Taryn Wood

DAD—Malcolm Callan

SHERRY—Cat Dean

OUTSIDERS—Deanna Moffitt

This play received development from Chicago Dramatists, Chicago, Illinois.

Cast of Characters

BOY SMALL and BOY GROWN, a 12-year-old boy and his spirit (played by a young adult)

SISSY, Boy's big sister, 14 (played by a young adult)

DAD, father of Boy and Sissy, 30s-40s

SHERRY, Dad's second wife, 30s-40s

OUTSIDERS, a female neighbor, a social worker, and a teacher, 30s-60s

Setting

Action occurs in Dad's bedroom, over several weeks in spring, from Tax Day to Flag Day. Additional scenes occur in a neutral space, and should be staged in or near the bedroom.

Time

The present, and a possible future.

Acknowledgments

This fictional play is dedicated to the memory of Christian Choate.

Quotation from "The Force that Through the Green Fuse Drives the Flower," from *The Poems of Dylan Thomas*, published by New Directions. Copyright © 1952, 1953 Dylan Thomas.

BOY SMALL

SCENE 1: WHO CAN UNDERSTAND

(In darkness. The silhouette of a large dog cage is just visible. Near it stands the dim shape of a man, BOY GROWN.)

BOY GROWN: Who can understand such suffering as mine? I'd put money on it, not a soul. Not even the Greeks. Two infants served up for their father's unwitting appetite? They go quick and into the pot. But mine's a slow pattern. Take Shakespeare. His Romeo and Juliet? Poison and a stab. His MacDuff and Lady M and Gertrude and Ophelia? Off this earth before the blood could dry. In their suffering, they had a measure of freedom. Or maybe we all see through the glass of our own predicament. I feel mine is the worst fate, but that's the way I see it. Okay, maybe Desdemona knew a little of my pain. That scene with the maid, all the questions? No. She at least had the novelty of fear where before was just lover's anticipation. You see I'm selfish in my suffering. Truly, I recognize no one's but my own. I am selfish. I belong here.

SISSY: Good.

BOY GROWN: I am self-centered.

SISSY: You totally are.

(Lights shift. BOY GROWN gets into cage and becomes BOY SMALL.)

BOY SMALL: But I really do gotta go to the bathroom.

SISSY: You just used it.

(Afternoon. The crowded but organized bedroom of a modular home. Boxes and bins stacked neatly. An electric guitar hangs on a wall. The only messy area is a dresser spilling jewelry and makeup.

SISSY stirs a noodle cup.)

BOY SMALL: I'm thirsty.

SISSY: There's water on the ramen.

BOY SMALL: Sissy.

SISSY: I can't. *(A beat.)* You are such a pain.

BOY SMALL: I know.

(SISSY unlocks the cage. BOY SMALL crawls out. He stretches; he's been in there a long time.)

SISSY: Hurry up.

BOY SMALL: Gotta get my parts shook out so it don't come out my nose.

SISSY: I'm coming with.

BOY SMALL: No one's home.

SISSY: I'm coming with or you don't go.

BOY SMALL: What for, you wanna watch?

SISSY: Gross.

(BOY dances and sings a made-up pop song.)

BOY SMALL: "Catch me, baby, you never can/Touch me, baby, in Neverland/You can try but I can fly…"

(DAD enters. SISSY and BOY freeze. DAD sets down his keys and wallet.)

SISSY: He was coming right back.

DAD: There's food getting cold.

(DAD exits.)

SISSY: I like a boy. Hey. Brother-boy. I have a crush on someone.

BOY SMALL: What does he smell like?

SISSY: I don't know. He has black hair. He's new. He said hi to me yesterday. And then today, too.

BOY SMALL: I wasn't running.

SISSY: You would have.

(SISSY gets her backpack, chooses a book. BOY sniffs the air.)

BOY SMALL: Some kind of meat.

SISSY: Maybe Jack-a-loaf! "Best burger…"

SISSY & BOY: "Or you don't know Jack!"

BOY SMALL: Nope. Pizza. Mmm, pepperoni.

(SISSY gives BOY a book.)

SISSY: The page is marked.

BOY SMALL: Ugh. Not algebra.

SISSY: Today he said hi, and he was like, what are you up to? And I said, nothing, what are you up to? And he said, nothing.

BOY SMALL: And you couldn't smell him.

SISSY: I don't know. Soap.

BOY SMALL: So, lathery? Flowery-deodorant-musky-melony? Citrusy-waterfall-cinnamon-sea breezy?

SISSY: No way. Not bringing him here.

BOY SMALL: You could. Early in the day.

SISSY: He doesn't know about us. I'd bring him to Mommy's.

BOY SMALL: Don't be stupid.

SISSY: You're the one.

BOY SMALL: I wasn't running.

SISSY: I'd bring him to Babylon. If I just had a couple dollars.

BOY SMALL: I must smell him to see if I approve.

SISSY: Just a twenty.

BOY SMALL: Gave you twenty last week.

SISSY: Ten, then.

BOY SMALL: You don't need money to hang out. Hang. Out.

SISSY: You're so mean. You're so unfair. I might not even like him. I might never want to hang out with him again. Probably I won't. I'll bring you something. Piece of pizza. I'll bring you a Jumbo bar. I'll bring you whatever you want.

BOY SMALL: Something he wears. A sock would be best.

SISSY: You goofball. How 'bout his underwear?

BOY SMALL: His underwear. I didn't.

SISSY: You want his underwear.

BOY SMALL: You do.

SISSY: You do!

BOY SMALL: Nuh-uh.

SISSY: Uh-huh.

DAD: *(Offstage)* Sissy!

BOY SMALL: Sh-h!

SISSY: Coming right now! Just getting his homework!

(DAD enters, tax form in one hand, piece of pizza in the other.)

DAD: Forget that.

BOY SMALL: No. I need it.

DAD: Thanks to you, I can't even eat.

BOY SMALL: Smells good.

DAD: *(To SISSY)* Take the book. Get in the kitchen.

BOY SMALL: You can't do that.

DAD: I can't? Get over there.

BOY SMALL: It's not fair.

(BOY kneels in his accustomed position for punishment, and DAD whips him with the belt.)

DAD: Oh, you call the shots? You wanna tell me? I'm out there working my ass off. You don't tell me.

(DAD tosses the belt aside. BOY sneaks DAD's wallet from the bedside table, takes a twenty.)

SISSY: It's my fault, I took too long.

DAD: What did I just tell you?

(SISSY exits, without book.)

DAD: Ain't even your book.

BOY SMALL: The books in my grade are stupid.

DAD: Maybe you're too smart for school.

BOY SMALL: I still want to go. Dad. Dad.

DAD: The gas money alone, driving around to hunt you down.

BOY SMALL: I know.

DAD: You don't know. One second, work is so slow I can't sleep. I can't think of nothing except is this the day they do it, the bastards. Then it picks up and I'm working 12-hour days in global fucking warming.

BOY SMALL: You look tired.

DAD: All of a sudden it's April 15 and I'll be up all night tonight, 'cause they don't even give you a day off. No. I gotta spend my own time trying to figure out how to get the government to gimme back my own money.

BOY SMALL: If it's too hard for you, I could do it.

(A beat.)

DAD: Why are you like this? Why can't you do one little thing to give me a minute of peace?

BOY SMALL: Dad, please. One more chance. I wouldn't run.

(DAD gestures to his piece of pizza.)

DAD: You can eat that.

(DAD exits with book.)

(BOY SMALL becomes BOY GROWN. During the following, he tosses pizza in trash and returns to cage.)

BOY GROWN: Bolingbroke is crossing the river, getting his Henry-the-Fourth name badge all ready, slapping his millions of soldiers on the ass and saying, pay you back man, come see me in the castle and I'll set you up. Good, good, you do that, Bolingbroke, but I'm gonna win. I will have my victory. Me and he who keeps his court right smack in the hollow crown that rounds the mortal temples of a king. He's my right-hand man. He's my ally. He's my strength. When you have time, real time like I have, all the years of all my futures, to spend just how I want, you can see what Shakespeare's talking about. You can see what the bible's talking about. You can see this whole conversation the world is having. Back and forth, like strings across a guitar. He never did play that guitar. I don't know why he kept it. But that was part of the conversation, it helped me to hear. It helped me to see how I will win. Me here, every moment, every action, winning.

(End of scene.)

SCENE 2: OUR LOVE IS PROUD

(A few days later. SHERRY enters, getting into her work uniform. BOY sits in cage.)

SHERRY: *(calls)* This is once-in-a-lifetime. Take it or leave it.

BOY SMALL: Better hurry up. You're gonna be late.

SHERRY: *(ignores BOY, calls)* Just getting to the finals. Just getting there.

(SHERRY waits but no reply.)

SHERRY: Don't tell me we wouldn't win. I know we would. We screw better than anyone else in the world, tell me you don't know that.

(DAD enters, working on a tax form.)

DAD: I don't need to prove to a bunch of strangers how good I fuck.

SHERRY: How good we fuck. You and me, how we do it. Just getting picked gets you a thousand dollars. I'm not even talking winning, I'm not even talking the finals.

DAD: Thousand. And how much goes to taxes.

SHERRY: Who cares, you already missed the filing date.

DAD: This pen won't write.

SHERRY: I got a pen. And look at this! Gets us to the front of the line. Guaranteed.

DAD: You blew money on a pass.

SHERRY: My tips.

DAD: Whose tips?

SHERRY: It's the one thing I'm good at.

DAD: Jesus.

SHERRY: Make fun if you want, go ahead. But. Does it not mean something that my one skill, my one God-given talent, does it not mean anything that it's finally being recognized on national TV? And don't say porn. Married sex is not porn.

DAD: "Watch out, fans. It's wa-a-a-y dirtier."

SHERRY: Go ahead, I don't care. It's just something I want. Something that matters to my heart of hearts. If it was her, it would all be different.

DAD: Why don't we have any pens.

SHERRY: Give her a son, give her a daughter, what do you give me? Dried-up pen. He smells, did he get washed?

DAD: *(calls)* Sissy!

SHERRY: Not home yet.

DAD: What time is it?

SHERRY: It eats at me. Having to look at his face and see her staring out. Looking all sweet and innocent when you know they got their eye somewhere else.

DAD: What are you saying?

SHERRY: Nothing.

DAD: You saying I got left.

SHERRY: I'm talking about him. Running to her every chance he gets.

DAD: At least she calls us.

SHERRY: And how she loves to call. I bet she eggs him on. She gets him to run, just so she has another reason to get you on the phone.

DAD: Well, he's not running now.

SHERRY: Point is, look what you did for her. And she's not even grateful. She just uses it to make trouble for you.

DAD: We don't know that was her.

SHERRY: Who else would call? 'Cross-the-street? Next door? They mind their business.

DAD: Could be 'Cross-the-street. Ever since she sold it to us, "Where's the dog, when you getting the dog."

SHERRY: If I knew when they're coming, I could borrow Karen's dog. Have it running around.

DAD: You would do that.

SHERRY: If they would just call first. If they could just make it a little easier on a person.

DAD: My good girl.

SHERRY: It's about me being proud. Wanting to show you off. Don't you see, she's not worthy of you. Look what she made you, his teeth aren't even straight, hands all buckled. Not like your hands.

DAD: What about my hands.

SHERRY: I love your hands. On me. I dream about them.

DAD: What for, I'm right here.

SHERRY: Day dream. At work. At the store. All the time.

DAD: You know that's my one day off.

SHERRY: Four hours max. We get down there, we got the pass, we're in front of the line, we do our thing, we blow them away. I don't care, I know we blow them away. And if we don't get picked we go home.

DAD: And if we do, a thousand bucks. More like seven hundred.

SHERRY: I know we get picked. I know we are sharing something sacred and hot, and any judge who can't see that should die.

DAD: I'll think about it. Think about it, I said. He does smell. You pee on yourself? You trying that now?

SHERRY: I'll tend to him.

DAD: It's her job. Where the hell is she?

SHERRY: Not important. I got it. Get a drink, give me the taxes.

DAD: It's my job.

SHERRY: It's no problem, I'll finish it on my break.

DAD: That supposed to be funny?

SHERRY: I want you to rest now. I want you to close your eyes. Think what you'll do with a thousand dollars. Seven hundred.

DAD: If that.

SHERRY: Motorcycle. Vacation. Down payment on a house.

DAD: You got no money sense.

SHERRY: I got dreams. Go get your beer.

(DAD exits. SHERRY hides the tax forms in her purse and gets ready for work.)

BOY SMALL: My hands are not buckled.

SHERRY: I've always hated pretty girls. They don't have to do anything but be pretty. But they act so superior, like they accomplished something. Congratulations on being born.

BOY SMALL: My mommy was pretty. She had long blond hair.

SHERRY: Your mommy had short hair. Short and butch.

BOY SMALL: Long and silky. The ends of it tickled my nose.

SHERRY: Where do you come up with this crap?

BOY SMALL: It was before you. She used to look at Daddy just like you do.

SHERRY: No one looks at him the way I do.

BOY SMALL: If you get on the show, I could help. I could be the fluffer.

SHERRY: You dirty brain. There's no fluffer. How do you know about a fluffer.

BOY SMALL: It's on the videos.

SHERRY: Watching when you're supposed to be sleeping.

BOY SMALL: Sometimes it's loud.

(SHERRY opens cage, sets out paper and pen.)

SHERRY: Get your mind dirty and you'll never get it clean. Boy, here. Paper. Homework. Why doesn't anyone like me.

BOY SMALL: Okay. Why doesn't anyone like you.

SHERRY: Like you, like *you*. Are you that stupid or do I get your daddy?

BOY SMALL: I am that stupid.

(SHERRY goes back to getting ready. BOY starts to write.)

BOY SMALL: "Why doesn't anyone…" Hey, this pen won't write.

SHERRY: So what, no one's going to read it. *(BOY is hurt.)* Oh geez, here. *(tosses BOY a pen.)*

BOY SMALL: *(almost in tears)* Forget it.

SHERRY: You dish it out, no problem. That's why no one likes you. You think you can live by two sets of rules, one for you and one for everyone else. Just like a pretty girl.

BOY SMALL: I want people to like me.

SHERRY: Then you gotta try harder.

BOY SMALL: Will you help me?

SHERRY: *(sighs)* Go get yourself a mint.

(BOY goes to dresser and takes a mint; also steals some money from her cocktail apron.)

SHERRY: I count my singles, you know.

BOY SMALL: Just looking for chocolate.

SHERRY: There's no chocolate. There's mints. That's enough, you get back now.

BOY SMALL: *(returns to cage area; hides the money)* Mm, starlights.

SHERRY: We probably don't even have a chance.

BOY SMALL: Of course you do.

SHERRY: You better not be watching.

BOY SMALL: 'Course not. I happen to think you have a great chance.

SHERRY: You do?

BOY SMALL: Sure. Sherry, look at you. You're so special and you're so smart, and... so easy.

SHERRY: You're sick, you know that?

BOY SMALL: No, seriously. Your technique is fine, but you're missing that something extra.

SHERRY: Sicko. Someone should wash your mouth out.

BOY SMALL: Someone really should.

(SHERRY starts to drag BOY to bathroom.)

SHERRY: You think I won't do it? *(Changes her mind)* Oh no, I'm not falling for that.

BOY SMALL: I won't run.

SHERRY: Damn right you won't. Get in there and I'll bring you the soap.

(BOY SMALL gets into cage. SHERRY locks him in and exits. BOY SMALL becomes BOY GROWN.)

BOY GROWN: The first few days are the hardest. Peanut butter and jelly, the way it squishes all sticky-slidy. My favorite burger. Teeth sinking into a soft bun. But that's normal. Just my brain, craving glucose. In a few days, the craving fades. My brain gets more determined. We all out of glycogen? No problem, we synthesize fats and proteins instead. The brain keeps going, all on its own. It moves on. It leeches acid waste from stored-up pizza sticks and taco tots. That's not the prettiest part, but acidosis is a great appetite suppressant. And the payoff? Normalization. That's where the blood chemistry corrects itself. My tissues and organs actually start to heal. It's amazing, what the brain knows how to do. Weeks go by, and it cleans the body of everything except vital tissue. It keeps readjusting to maximize reserves. Except of course, if you don't have reserves. If the food you eat doesn't have actual food in it, well, that speeds up the amazingness.

(End of scene.)

SCENE 3: PARENTING

(A few days later. DAD enters, SISSY behind him, carrying her backpack.)

SISSY: I swear. I had to stay late.

DAD: I call over there right now, that's what they'll say.

SISSY: Yes. Of course.

(SHERRY enters. She gets her purse and prepares for work.)

SHERRY: Office is closed by now.

DAD: Who were you talking to.

SISSY: No one. I was helping with the bulletin boards.

SHERRY: Ha.

SISSY: I was. Please Daddy I was. You can call the school tomorrow. Ask Miss Carmen.

DAD: You know the rules.

SISSY: I didn't talk to anyone. I never said anything.

DAD: *(gets belt)* Four o'clock is the rule.

SISSY: *(kneels at bed, preparing to be hit)* I didn't know it was so late. I swear I didn't.

DAD: You go off giving it to some boy—

SISSY: I wasn't.

DAD: And you know what you end up with? This.

(DAD offers belt to SISSY.)

SISSY: Huh?

DAD: Come on, let's make sure you can do it.

SHERRY: Do what?

DAD: *(to SISSY)* You think it's easy taking care of a kid?

SISSY: You mean...

(DAD opens cages, motions to BOY.)

DAD: Get over there.

(SISSY stands. BOY takes SISSY's place, kneeling at the bed. DAD demonstrates.)

DAD: Fold it over. You want the buckle at the thumb side. Bend your arm. And that's where you want the buckle. Any longer and you hit yourself. Don't want to be doing that.

(SISSY follows instructions.)

DAD: Stand solid, feet farther apart. Step that foot forward, that's where you hold your weight. Good. Now when you swing it, you want it to go diagonal, top to bottom, like you're making an X.

(SISSY makes an half-hearted attempt to whip BOY.)

DAD: Try again.

(SISSY tries harder. BOY flinches.)

DAD: Better. Make the X the other way. Good. Seems hard to you now, but it just gets harder. The older you get, the more people counting on you, the more people watching you.

SHERRY: I don't know about this.

DAD: Hey. What are you doing next Saturday.

SHERRY: Next Saturday? You don't mean...

DAD: It's her chore now. He don't do his exercise, he don't eat, he tries anything, she knows what to do.

SHERRY: Wait. Are you telling me . . ?

DAD: *(to SISSY)* You keep the door locked. You don't leave the key in the deadbolt.

SISSY: I hide the key.

SHERRY: Oh my God. Oh my God. What am I gonna wear.

DAD: What did we learn?

SISSY: I do my chores.

DAD: When do you do them?

SISSY: Four o'clock.

DAD: Sherry's gonna be late for work now.

SISSY: It will never happen again.

SHERRY: I had to give him his food, not that he ate it. First it wasn't warm enough. Then it was too hot. I'm back and forth to the microwave a million times, with 'Cross-the-street out there on patrol.

SISSY: She asked again, when I came in.

DAD: Jesus. "Where's the dog? When you gonna get the dog?"

SHERRY: I can talk to Karen.

DAD: Yeah, ask her.

SHERRY: 'Text her right now.

DAD: Gonna see her at work.

SHERRY: It's ten cents.

DAD: Unless you're over, then it's seventy-five.

SHERRY: I'm not over. I mean, how am I supposed to know if I'm over? Half my texts I don't even get. Then they all come at once. Karen has this thing where it doesn't even go through a text thing, we should have that.

DAD: In your own little world.

SISSY: *(to BOY)* Come on. Let's do your pushups. One. *(BOY does a pushup.)* Two.

(BOY does a second pushup. DAD watches SISSY.)

SHERRY: *(to DAD)* I gotta go.

DAD: Hold on.

SISSY: Three. Come on.

(SISSY snaps belt. BOY does a third pushup.)

SHERRY: She's got it.

(SHERRY and DAD exit.)

SISSY: Four. *(BOY does fourth pushup. She clears her throat; he rests.)* Five. Six.

BOY SMALL: *(whispers)* Did you see him?

SISSY: *(nods; full voice)* Seven. Eight. *(whispers)* We went to Babylon. Nine! He said, what are you up to and I said not much what are you up to? And we just went.

BOY SMALL: I bet you spent the whole twenty.

SISSY: It's my money. *(Snaps the belt, a little vindictively)* Nine! Do it. *(BOY does it.)* Ten. *(He does another pushup; it's hard for him.)* Ten, good! Now your sit-ups. One! Two! *(whispers)* It was so fun. We talked. I mean, not about anything you know, but we just hung out, and we got freezy-bombs, and I bought, and I did not spend it all. But I could of.

BOY SMALL: You could've.

SISSY: But I didn't. I want to have lots more times. Just like that time. And I got you a surprise, weirdo. *(Opens her backpack; full voice)* Now you gotta eat.

(Whispers) No way was I asking for a sock. *(Gives BOY a baseball cap.)*

BOY SMALL: You are the best sister in the world.

SISSY: You want ramen or coco-pops?

BOY SMALL: Will you tell Mommy...

SISSY: Stop asking me.

BOY SMALL: I mean this Mommy. Tell her you fed me.

SISSY: But I haven't even—

BOY SMALL: Just say I ate. Do it, and I'll give you a ten.

SISSY: You have to be hungry. What is your problem?

(BOY sniffs the hat.)

BOY SMALL: I don't smell anything.

SISSY: *(reaches for hat)* What do you mean? Let me see.

BOY SMALL: *(clutches it to him)* No. Mine.

SISSY: Then give me the money.

(BOY digs into hiding place in his cage and gets out money for SISSY.)

(End of scene.)

SCENE 4: NEIGHBORLY

(NEIGHBOR enters. Her entrance defines a neutral space, separate from the bedroom, which represents her home and then the street outside. She seems to watch BOY counting out money for SISSY. She addresses us.)

NEIGHBOR: Something over there ain't right. It's not my business. Maybe I shouldn't be calling. I'm nosy. My pop said it, now my daughter says it. She says, what you need is another dog. I said, why? When I die you gonna get another Ma? Henry wasn't a dog. He was Henry.

(SISSY exits. NEIGHBOR seems to watch her.)

NEIGHBOR: I see the girl going back and forth. I used to see the boy. Lately I never see the boy. Maybe there wasn't a boy. Maybe he didn't live there. Do I have to give my name? And the man. Something not right about him. Used to be an A-hole, now he's all neighborly.

DAD: *(enters)* Hey, neighbor!

NEIGHBOR: Hey, neighbor.

DAD: Warm for April. Global warming, right?

NEIGHBOR: Right. *(to us)* Probably wonders what else I got to get rid of. My dog Henry was one hundred percent Bernese. My daughter kept saying Bur-MEEZ. I said Bur-NEEZ, Bur-NEEZ, oughta call him Bernie so you remember. But Henry's what we went with. *(to DAD)* Perfect puppy weather.

DAD: Yeah?

NEIGHBOR: For taking them out, yeah. Don't want to be starting all that in the winter, right?

DAD: Got that right.

NEIGHBOR: So when you getting him? When you getting the dog?

DAD: Soon.

NEIGHBOR: Henry loved that crate.

DAD: Yep, you told me.

NEIGHBOR: Yeah, even after he got housebroken. Every night, ten o'clock, he'd go stand by the door. He was so polite, Mr. French my dad called him. He said, you should've called that dog--

DAD: Shoulda called him Mr. French, yeah.

NEIGHBOR: He'd stand there and look at me and I'd go, Okay Henry, go to bed. And he'd go in there and curl up and go right to sleep.

DAD: Yeah, dogs are great.

NEIGHBOR: When you getting one? I keep hoping I'm gonna look out and see the dog.

DAD: I look out, all I see is this darned trash. It's terrible.

NEIGHBOR: Terrible. They just throw it out the windows.

DAD: Throw it out, world is their trashcan. Lucky we got people like you around, always keeping an eye on things. Kids better watch out for you.

NEIGHBOR: That's just me. How many you got again?

DAD: Huh?

NEIGHBOR: Kids.

DAD: Let's see, that I know of? Ha, ha.

NEIGHBOR: *(jokes)* Uh-oh, steer clear of that one. *(DAD exits)* After he passed, I couldn't look at that damned crate. I gave them the whole thing for practically nothing. But that's not why. I mean, I was happy to do it. I don't want bad feelings. But, he was the best listener, the way he'd look in your eyes. My daughter said yeah he's listening for Bacon Henry, Cheese Henry. She told me not to call. None of your business, Ma. Get a dog, Ma, keep you out of trouble. But if I did, I don't even have a crate. I guess that's why I did it. Yeah. In honor of Henry. So I won't be tempted, you know? ... Yeah. I can hold.

(NEIGHBOR exits.)

(End of scene.)

SCENE 5: GIRLS DAY OUT

(A few days later. BOY is in cage. SISSY and SHERRY enter, each carrying fancy shopping bags brimming with teddies, negligees, slip dresses.)

SISSY: I love the blue one.

SHERRY: It's not too short?

SISSY: Not at all. Your legs look amazing in that.

SHERRY: Better than the two-piece one?

SISSY: Did I see the two-piece one?

SHERRY: I'll try it on.

(SHERRY looks through various bags. SISSY unlocks BOY's cage.)

SISSY: Come on, let's do your business.

(BOY crawls out. SHERRY pulls out a pink garment.)

SHERRY: Oh I forgot this one. I thought I didn't buy this.

SISSY: I love that one.

SHERRY: I've never been a pink person.

SISSY: You could wear anything. With a French manicure oh my god. *(to BOY)* Come on.

SHERRY: Is the front door locked?

SISSY: Yes. Key's not in it.

SHERRY: I'll check.

SISSY: I hid the key.

(SHERRY exits.)

BOY SMALL: How could you stand it?

SISSY: It wasn't so bad. We went all over Babylon, in every store. She just kept pulling out her card, buying and buying.

BOY SMALL: You smell.

SISSY: They spray you for free.

BOY SMALL: *(holds his nose)* It's like flower needles.

SHERRY: *(entering)* Okay, go ahead. Hurry up.

SISSY: *(leads BOY out)* I got some of them on little cards. Just 'cause I was with her.

SHERRY: *(holds a garment up to herself)* "Couple number one, speaking for all the judges, I have to tell you that you really brought it. Everyone was amazingly talented, but you two brought something to the table that I have to say, blew us away." "Oh, thank you, it's just kind of the way we always do it." "Wow. I thought I knew what married sex was all about. But I speak for all of us, the entire audience, the entire world, when I say that you are going to Regionals!"

(BOY and SISSY have returned. SISSY, carrying BOY's ramen cup, cheers wildly.)

SISSY: And then they hand you the check.

SHERRY: I don't care about that.

BOY SMALL: You will when the VISA bill comes.

SISSY: Eat your food.

(SHERRY continues unpacking purchases.)

SHERRY: Just like your father. A thousand is nothing. You get through regionals, you get to finals, and I'm talking ten grand, plus they do news stories, interviews, everything opens up.

BOY SMALL: Opening up, he'll love that.

SISSY: Eat.

BOY SMALL: I'll do my stuff first.

(BOY does some desultory exercises.)

SHERRY: Here's the black one.

(SHERRY changes into black garment.)

SISSY: Ooh, I didn't see that one. You got so many. You're so lucky.

SHERRY: Get a job, get a credit card.

SISSY: I've asked.

SHERRY: I didn't say to ask. Jesus, where am I gonna hide all these.

SISSY: Hide them?

SHERRY: Maybe your room. Unless… he comes in there.

SISSY: Not in my room.

SHERRY: No?

SISSY: Hardly. Not when I'm there.

SHERRY: Oh.

SISSY: Why?

SHERRY: I don't know. *(Answers earlier question)* In case he says, Why you buying all those, blah blah.

SISSY: Oh Sherry… You look so beautiful.

SHERRY: Yeah? Get the tags off.

SISSY: With red nails and big silver hoops. I like your hair down, but I like it up too.

SHERRY: I'm thinking, if I go with the black I'll get red lowlights. But if I go with the blue, or that teal one, I don't know. Get them off.

(SISSY carefully cuts the tags off the garments as SHERRY unwraps them.)

SISSY: You look so young in the teal one. Like my age. Blond highlights if you do that one, right? And silver shadow.

SHERRY: *(holds the teal garment up to herself)* There's this facial now called a Shimmer. It's half-price if you order it with a derm, but you don't do it when you get the derm.

SISSY: Derm is like a peel?

SHERRY: You have to do that every two weeks or there's no point. Your pores just grow back.

SISSY: I bet my pores are huge.

SHERRY: Didn't your mom teach you anything? Here. Try on the pink.

SISSY: Oh, no.

SHERRY: You have to learn, if you want to do anything with men, how to handle them. Let them think they're in control yes, but… You think I tell him what I do all day? Every place I go?

BOY SMALL: You sure tell him enough.

SHERRY: Little tip. Tell them so many details they stop listening. Then they don't know what you told 'em. Hurry up, try it on. We'll hear the car.

(SISSY exits with pink negligee.)

BOY SMALL: I advise against the teal.

SHERRY: I should tell your dad what you say to me.

BOY SMALL: You should. But then you'd never get my secret special tips for victory.

SHERRY: Your secret tips, right.

BOY SMALL: I'll tell you how to win for one hundred dollars.

SHERRY: Ha!

BOY SMALL: Fifty. Twenty dollars. Come on, ten dollars.

SHERRY: What do you think you're gonna do with money?

BOY SMALL: It's not about sex, you know.

SHERRY: It's Married Sex. It's the whole point.

BOY SMALL: Sex is just the thing. Like the singing shows. Yeah you got to do it good, but you need more.

SHERRY: I got an entry pass, fourteen outfits, a shimmer facial, and a positive attitude. I got plenty.

(SISSY enters in pink negligee.)

SISSY: Feels weird.

SHERRY: You keep that.

SISSY: I couldn't.

SHERRY: No. You keep it. You're beautiful.

(In their negligees, SHERRY and SISSY hug.)

BOY SMALL: She can't wear that.

SISSY: *(gathers the shopping bags)* We can keep them under my bed.

BOY SMALL: You wouldn't wear that. Sissy?

SISSY: *(busy with bags)* Huh?

BOY SMALL: Hey, I'm not eating this ramen cup. Hey, what about my homework? I want poetry.

SISSY: *(tosses BOY her backpack.)* Poetry. There's some in here. *(to SHERRY)* Maybe we should save the tags.

SHERRY: God no. They need to go in the outside garbage.

SISSY: I can do that.

SHERRY: See how easy?

(SISSY and SHERRY begin to exit. BOY pulls out a book, pages through it.)

BOY SMALL: Hey, Sissy, hey. Poetry for Today. *(Clears throat dramatically)* "The force that through the green fuse drives the flower, drives my green age."

SISSY and SHERRY: Whatever.

(SISSY and SHERRY exit.

BOY SMALL becomes BOY GROWN. He throws his ramen cup in the garbage.)

BOY GROWN: "The force that through the green fuse," Yes. But what can that mean to Sissy? So removed from forces that would nourish her, all she sees is the one fluorescent light buzzing above her head. She seeks it, meristem feeling its way, but the green is wrong. Green with eyeliner, green with lash envy, green with Shamrock Shakes that only mean Easter is coming. They take away even her knowledge that she is ignorant, and they wrap her in padding. They who are they? Just the people making a buck to feed their family. They pad her fineness and her possibilities with the fats, the mood eveners, the entertainments, that render her redundant. She trundles through her day, unaware of photosynthesis, unaware of insect colonies, unaware of the miracle of her own anatomy. Of course teenage girls get pregnant. Of course preteen girls get pregnant. They're reaching for the light. They're reaching for one touch of the elemental fire. *(Returns to cage, becomes BOY SMALL)* Also, their boyfriends are jackasses.

(End of scene.)

SCENE 6: SISSY WANTS A DEAL

(A day later. SISSY enters holding a candy bar.)

SISSY: Surprise! I got you a Jumbo bar.

BOY SMALL: Sleeping.

SISSY: It's family size.

BOY SMALL: What do you want.

SISSY: Nothing. Could use a couple dollars.

BOY SMALL: Gave you five yesterday.

SISSY: What are you saving for? Not like you can spend it.

BOY SMALL: It's none of your business. Here. *(Digs in his stash and gives SISSY money.)*

SISSY: *(offers candy bar)* Thanks.

BOY SMALL: Keep your candy bar.

SISSY: Just have a little. You gotta eat something.

BOY SMALL: Tell her I did.

SISSY: He's asking.

BOY SMALL: He noticed. Good.

SISSY: You could give him a chance. Sometimes it's like you bring it on yourself.

BOY SMALL: What?

SISSY: You know what he wants and you do the opposite.

BOY SMALL: It's called free will. You wouldn't understand.

SISSY: You're the one stuck in there.

BOY SMALL: So.

SISSY: So why not make it easier on yourself.

BOY SMALL: Easier on you, you mean.

SISSY: On everyone. Just do what he wants. Why not? He'll let you out. He'll let you go back to school.

BOY SMALL: You think that.

SISSY: Miss Carmen asks about you every week.

BOY SMALL: She used to ask every day.

SISSY: She still talks about how smart you are. What a big brain you are. "He's one of the special ones." I was like, uh you could call it that. *(Eats the candy bar.)*

BOY SMALL: Sorry to be a pain.

SISSY: I didn't say that.

BOY SMALL: It's what you're thinking. Buckle down so I can get off guard duty. I'll get to go see Brendan-

Ethan. Or is it Ethan-Brendan. What's the point of two names? Why doesn't he pick one?

SISSY: You don't even know him.

BOY SMALL: *(gets the hat)* There's something about him I don't trust. Smell his hat.

SISSY: Ew-w.

BOY SMALL: I don't like that it doesn't smell like hair, even just a little.

SISSY: He's very clean.

BOY SMALL: Like Dad.

SISSY: He's nothing like Dad.

BOY SMALL: How come you always buy the freezy-bombs.

SISSY: I don't. I like to do things for him. It's not like Sherry.

BOY SMALL: I didn't mention Sherry.

SISSY: She's out of her mind about Daddy.

BOY SMALL: She likes to do things for him.

SISSY: You could just do what he says.

BOY SMALL: It wouldn't change anything.

SISSY: If you would act normal you could get out of there and then I wouldn't have to baby-sit you, and then maybe I could have a normal life.

BOY SMALL: Normal. Hanging out with Brendan-Ethan-Robot.

SISSY: You're just jealous. You don't want me to be happy.

BOY SMALL: I want you to be you. I want you to not end up with someone like Dad. Come on, smell this and tell me he's normal.

SISSY: You don't know anything.

BOY SMALL: I know you.

SISSY: No you don't.

BOY SMALL: I know everything about you. I know your favorite color, your favorite candy, your favorite ugly shoes. I know how many freckles you got on your back—

SISSY: Stop that.

BOY SMALL: Seventeen! Remember when I thought it was eighteen but one of them was a zit? It was so gross, it popped and you were—

SISSY: Don't ever talk about my back.

BOY SMALL: Why not?

SISSY: It's not. I'm your big sister.

BOY SMALL: So?

SISSY: You need to grow up.

BOY SMALL: Okay. I'll start by telling Dad what you've been up to.

SISSY: You would not.

BOY SMALL: Dad's house. Dad's rules.

SISSY: You know what he'd do.

BOY SMALL: Keep you from doing what you're not supposed to.

SISSY: Get over there.

BOY SMALL: I'd only do it to protect you.

SISSY: *(gets belt)* Do it. Don't you dare tell me what I can do and can't do. I love Brendan-Ethan and he is not like Daddy one bit, and if you make me be like Daddy I'll never forgive you.

BOY SMALL: I'm sorry. I won't tell.

SISSY: Damn right you won't. Don't worry, I'll tell them you ate.

(SISSY uses SHERRY's brush. Tries on a lipstick.)

BOY SMALL: Sissy-girl.

SISSY: He is nothing like Daddy. He's normal. He's nice. He has a grandma. She made me popcorn. And he didn't even want any.

BOY SMALL: Sounds like you should go out with his grandma.

SISSY: You're sick. You're a pervert. Give me my hat back.

BOY SMALL: Sissy.

SISSY: Stop making noise.

(SISSY puts on hat and exits.)

(End of scene.)

SCENE 7: MARRIED SEX

(A few days later. Afternoon. SHERRY and DAD enter, wearing light coats.)

DAD: Don't blame me.

(No answer from SHERRY. She takes off her coat, under which she is wearing the teal slip. DAD takes off his jacket. Underneath he's wearing jeans and a decent shirt.)

DAD: The whole thing was a joke. It's nothing like they show on TV. Four hours, bullshit. Lot of good your pass did. Who cares if you're in front of the line when all you're doing is standing there all day. And when we finally got in, the way you were jumping around. You looked desperate.

SHERRY: I was being vivacious.

DAD: We should have said we were brother and sister, that would've got them.

(SHERRY takes off the teal negligee and changes into sweats.)

SHERRY: You barely said anything.

DAD: They call it reality. They don't want reality. They want fake, like everyone else. Everyone who got the red-hot ticket, none of them were what they say they want—committed married couples.

SHERRY: They had something extra.

DAD: Like your costume? That thing makes everyone notice your neck.

SHERRY: What's wrong with my neck.

DAD: Usually you don't notice it cause of your hair. But today. I don't know, it was like it was glowing. Fuck that show. You don't need them. Take that thing back to the store, get the money back. Don't even tell me what you paid for the pass.

SHERRY: I can't return it.

DAD: The hell you can't. I don't want to see that thing.

SHERRY: Sissy liked it.

DAD: You let her see this trash? Don't give her ideas. Don't corrupt my little girl.

SHERRY: She is not a little girl. *(DAD cracks SHERRY, a medium hit. DAD continues changing. He neatly folds his shirt.)* Sorry. *(Pause.)* What else is wrong with me.

DAD: In your own little world.

SHERRY: Why would you even want me, with my neck right here.

DAD: Poor little dream girl, sh-h…

SHERRY: I wore it for you. It made me feel pretty.

DAD: So you got your money's worth. Cheer up. Just get rid of it. *(jokes)* Maybe save it for Sissy.

SHERRY: What?

DAD: Few years, she'll look good in it.

SHERRY: How can you say that. You just said.

DAD: Couple years makes a difference.

SHERRY: So a couple years ago, I would've looked good?

DAD: That's why I love you. You don't know the first thing about yourself.

(He undresses her. Doorbell BUZZES. They freeze, listen. BOY continues to sleep. Doorbell BUZZES a second time. SISSY enters.)

SISSY: There's a white car outside. Just a regular car.

DAD: *(to SISSY)* Get him out of there. At the table. Two of them at the table. *(Shoves a shirt at SHERRY.)* Put this on. Make sandwiches.

(SISSY lets BOY out of cage. He is groggy, comes out slowly. Doorbell BUZZES a third time. SISSY pulls BOY gently.)

SISSY: Hurry.

DAD: Don't be stupid. Whatever happens, whoever it is, they'll be gone in a minute and it will be us again.

BOY SMALL: *(weak)* My legs feel funny.

(DAD throws a blanket over the cage.)

DAD: *(to SHERRY)* Make a can of soup. He's got a cold. Both of them have a cold. Sissy.

SISSY: I have a cold.

DAD: Go.

(SHERRY, SISSY and BOY exit. Dad finishes hiding cage and exits as doorbell BUZZES a fourth time.

SOCIAL WORKER enters in a rush, carrying a large purse stuffed with forms and a clipboard. Her entrance defines a neutral space which represents the front entrance and then other parts of the house. She addresses us.)

SOCIAL WORKER: Children's Protective Services: Home visit, Saturday, May seventh, in response to a hotline call citing suspected child neglect. I know this report is late. They're all late. I'm typing in my car, on lunch, in a parking lot. And this is a good day. I just made huge progress with a very young family. Last time I was there we had roaches, bedbugs, and the two year-old had a bolt—a bolt!—in his mouth. I told them, I'm not seeing progress. They said, please, you're a wake-up call. Give us one more chance. And I go back this morning, and the trash is still waist-high, but the two-year-old? Had had a bath!

DAD: Nothing personal, but if you have some ID.

SOCIAL WORKER: Of course. Condition of home: Commensurate with similar homes in the area, a trailer park—delete—mobile home community. No immediate safety hazards. Small amount of missing siding. At least there is siding. Another client, the mom has her little girls living in the car because she got some sign that God is attacking them through the microwave. Usually it's demons attacking but whatever. *(suddenly remembering)* That psych evaluation should be back by now, why isn't that back yet?

DAD: Just curious, is it normal to come on a Saturday?

SOCIAL WORKER: Sorry. Quite a backlog.

DAD: No problem at all. Just can't think who would've called. A neighbor? Or, wasn't my ex, was it?

SOCIAL WORKER: I'm sorry, we can't.

DAD: Doesn't matter. Come on in.

SOCIAL WORKER: Occupants: Father aged 41, daughter aged 14, son aged 12, and father's second wife aged 42. No animals at this time.

DAD: I thought we'd go to the shelter and get a mutt, that's what I always had growing up, but they want a purebred.

SISSY: We do. We want a purebred.

DAD: So, we got some more saving to do.

SOCIAL WORKER: Cleanliness of home: No garbage on floor. No signs of infestation. Size of home: kitchen, bathroom, two bedrooms?

DAD: Plus the living room, that's where we sleep.

SOCIAL WORKER: I didn't note a bed.

DAD: Yeah, we need to get into a bigger place, but right now, way the economy is, I just feel lucky to have a job.

SOCIAL WORKER: Work situation appears stable.

DAD: Let me write down my boss's number, the address, whatever you need.

SOCIAL WORKER: Atmosphere of home: Voices at a moderate level. Children somewhat quiet, but it was reported that they have colds.

(SHERRY feels BOY's forehead.)

SHERRY: Feels like his temp is down a little.

SOCIAL WORKER: Concern demonstrated, appropriate care given.

SHERRY: Eat this, and then you two go back to bed. You know, I hate to say this but I think I'm getting it too.

DAD: Worst thing is, I think I brought it home.

SHERRY: If we just knew you were coming.

DAD: Not important. Finish your soup, kids. Hon, you maybe better go take some cold medicine.

SHERRY: Is that okay, can I?

SOCIAL WORKER: 'Tis the season.

(SHERRY enters bedroom, clears her dressing table of makeup, etc.)

SOCIAL WORKER: As part of this assessment, the biological mother was contacted. She currently resides with a man with whom she has one child, aged seven months. A joint custody agreement is in place and is here attached. No complaints on file regarding custody. Physical condition of the children: Daughter appears of average weight for her height. Boy appears slightly underweight.

DAD: I think he shot up, was it two and a half or three inches in this past year? Was it three?

(They wait but BOY doesn't answer.)

SISSY: It was. It was three inches exactly.

DAD: When I was his age, kinda went through the same thing. But since we started home-schooling, I think—

SOCIAL WORKER: Home schooling? *(checks form)* There's nothing...

DAD: We started that in January, the January term. I'll talk to you about that, uh, in a minute, but I tell you, we started him in sixth, and he blew through it so fast we bought the seventh grade curriculum.

SOCIAL WORKER: That's very impressive. You passed the standardized sixth-grade battery?

BOY SMALL: No.

DAD: Not yet, of course not. Standardized test, end of the term, right?

(Pause.)

SISSY: Good soup.

DAD: You kids go get better now.

(SISSY and BOY exit.)

SOCIAL WORKER: When the son and daughter were not present, father informed me that the son had a situation.

DAD: Older boys, he wouldn't tell me their names, but I remember that age, it can make things worse. And I'm sure not a teacher, but everyone talks about this home schooling.

SHERRY: *(entering)* I never thought I'd be happy to work a night shift, but it means I'm able to be home with him.

DAD: She goes through his lessons, checks his work.

SHERRY: I just follow the curriculum.

DAD: She's being modest, she puts a lot into it.

(Meanwhile, in bedroom, SISSY has helped BOY into bed. She pulls the baseball cap from her pocket.)

SISSY: *(quietly)* Wear this.

BOY SMALL: What for.

SISSY: I don't know. Make you look more normal.

BOY SMALL: Get it away from me.

SISSY: There's nothing wrong with it. It's a normal hat.

BOY SMALL: With no smell? I bet he doesn't even exist. You made him up.

(Meanwhile, in the kitchen, the adults stand politely.)

SOCIAL WORKER: May I see the children's rooms?

SHERRY: I hope Sissy cleaned her room.

(SOCIAL WORKER, DAD, and SHERRY exit.)

SISSY: He loves me. He's gonna get me out of here.

BOY SMALL: One word from me could get you out right this second. Five minutes from now we're in that white car, speeding away.

SISSY: Can they do that?

BOY SMALL: She'd probably only take me. You're so happy here. "Good soup!"

SISSY: You would leave me here?

BOY SMALL: You were a jerk.

SISSY: So say something.

BOY SMALL: You say something.

SISSY: You're so brave, why don't you?

BOY SMALL: Maybe I will.

SISSY: Will not.

BOY SMALL: Will so.

SHERRY: Sissy, you should be in bed. These two are thick as thieves.

SOCIAL WORKER: And this is your room?

DAD: Yep, this is his room.

SOCIAL WORKER: *(pleasantly)* I'm asking him. Colds are yucky. Do you get a lot of colds? Might want to put a vaporizer in here. That looks like a fancy guitar. Are you a musician?

DAD: He's really talen—Oh! *(Covers his mouth)* My bad.

(SOCIAL WORKER examines boxes.)

SOCIAL WORKER: Lots of boxes. Do you do your schoolwork in here?

SHERRY: Right here at this— *(covers her mouth)* I'm so sorry.

(SOCIAL WORKER pulls blanket from cage.)

SOCIAL WORKER: Is this for the purebred?

(Pause. All watch BOY.)

BOY SMALL: Don't touch my stuff.

SOCIAL WORKER: Conclusion: Standard indicators of home safety, children's health, and inter-family dynamics appear within normal range.

DAD: *(to BOY)* You did good.

(End of scene.)

SCENE 8: JACK-A-LOAF TIME

(A week later. BOY remains on bed. SOCIAL WORKER continues report. SHERRY and SISSY deliver a fast food bag and report to DAD as they exit. DAD reads report.)

SOCIAL WORKER: Recommendation: Case ticket to remain open for six— SIX! I have six more reports to write up, and I need to be in court. And that psych evaluation. And my sandwich. Where's my sandwich? I forgot my sandwich. Case ticket to remain open for six months, pending 90-day re-check of standard indicators...

DAD: Indicators, we aced those.

SOCIAL WORKER: And pending sixth grade battery results.

DAD: A test, you can ace that.

SOCIAL WORKER: And pending confirmation from school district that notification to home school was properly filed.

(SOCIAL WORKER exits.)

DAD: Fucking fascist system. I gotta ask them if it's okay to educate my own— Fine, we'll get through it. Just gotta get you ready for that test. June fifteen. Got a couple weeks. You learned your lesson. Right?

(DAD takes a wrapped burger out of the bag.)

BOY SMALL: Jack-a-loaf?

DAD: "Best burger…"

BOY SMALL: "…Or you don't know Jack."

DAD: Went and got some dinner for the men. Line at the drive-through, I was ready to set my car on fire. These fat-asses can't get out of their little bubbles and go up to the counter. They should save the drive-through for people in a hurry. That's what it's for. So eat it.

BOY SMALL: I'll eat in just a little bit.

DAD: I want to see you take a bite.

BOY SMALL: It smells… dead.

DAD: Cooked fine.

(DAD forces the burger into BOY's mouth. BOY tries to chew.)

DAD: See that? It's good. Meat on your bones. *(BOY swallows with difficulty.)* Another.

BOY SMALL: I can't.

(BOY and DAD struggle.)

DAD: You're gonna get better. Gonna eat. Quit running.

BOY SMALL: I ain't running.

DAD: And you get rewarded. See?

(BOY takes the burger.)

BOY SMALL: I show you I'm better and you let me out.

DAD: You think I like this? Giving up my privacy. Giving up my time. Doesn't have to be like this.

BOY SMALL: No?

DAD: Another bite.

(BOY appears to take another bite.)

BOY SMALL: I get better. I go back to school.

DAD: It's where you belong.

BOY SMALL: You let me.

DAD: You show me.

BOY SMALL: Be around people.

DAD: You keep your mouth shut.

BOY SMALL: I keep my mouth shut.

DAD: You keep your mouth shut. You prove you keep your mouth shut. Prove it to me.

BOY SMALL: I prove it how.

DAD: They try to get around you. The counselors. Some of the teachers. Especially the women.

BOY SMALL: I don't talk to them.

DAD: Any woman out there will mother a child. What they don't tell you, she don't care what child.

BOY SMALL: Not Mommy.

DAD: You don't need her. You got twenty more just like her every time you turn around. They'll mother anything. A kid. A purse. Jesus, some of these purses. Before you know it, they're knocking on my door. Everyone out there, they all know better.

BOY SMALL: It could change.

DAD: Nothing changes.

(DAD sits on bed.)

BOY SMALL: But, Dad. If it did. If things could be different.

DAD: Huh?

BOY SMALL: Just for a second, say it could change.

DAD: What for.

BOY SMALL: Just, I don't know. For fun. What would you do?

DAD: I'd go back.

BOY SMALL: Back to when. When you were a kid?

DAD: Not that far. Back to before this. You and Sissy and Mommy and money and bullshit. I'd get my Strat, and I'd go on the road. And I'd jam.

BOY SMALL: Yeah?

DAD: Yeah.

BOY SMALL: Play it.

DAD: Huh?

BOY SMALL: I wish you'd play it. I bet you sound good.

DAD: You little shit, you're not even swallowing. How can I trust you to go to school. How can I trust you for one second.

BOY SMALL: I didn't tell. I never told.

DAD: About what.

BOY SMALL: About… you know. *(pause)* About nothing.

(DAD lies back on bed.)

DAD: Twenty-four hours in a day, seven days in a week. And you here, every second, a time bomb.

BOY SMALL: What about what you said. School and…

DAD: We'll see. *(Sighs)* You can't swallow one bite. How can I let you back with all those people.

BOY SMALL: We'll see.

DAD: Jesus. I don't know. I'm tired.

(DAD falls asleep.)

BOY SMALL: It's okay. We're almost there. A few days maybe.

(BOY SMALL becomes BOY GROWN, remains on bed with DAD.)

BOY GROWN: It's a secret place. It's this place where Tom's of Maine and Burt of Burt's Bees used to meet up. A little town called Crabtree and Evelyn. I'll chop and set you a cord of wood in return for room and board. Casually, Burt mentions that he's found a place where the sweetest fennel grows, and Tom offers a chess lesson in return. I'm quiet there. I tag along. I learn to live off the land. The sky is very blue and the birds wisp-wisp in the morning.

(SISSY enters, wearing the hat and stirring a cup of ramen noodles. She pauses when she sees DAD.)

BOY SMALL: We ate already.

SISSY: Jack-a-loaf?

BOY SMALL: You didn't get one. Just me.

SISSY: I don't want a gross burger.

(SISSY eats from the ramen cup; watches DAD.)

SISSY: I said I was sorry.

BOY SMALL: Good for you.

SISSY: Fine. I'm not sorry.

BOY SMALL: Same, same, all the same.

SISSY: Do your exercises.

BOY SMALL: Yes, Ma'am.

(BOY gathers his strength and prepares to do a push-up.)

SISSY: One. Two.

(BOY is unable to continue.)

SISSY: Come on… Three. Don't be a jerk, do it.

(BOY collapses.)

SISSY: Real funny. You really want to be like this.

BOY SMALL: So punish me.

SISSY: This is not fair. It's not fair of you to do this to me. You don't even care what I'm going through. You have no idea.

BOY SMALL: Aw, really, Dad? You got it rough.

SISSY: Fine. Over there.

(BOY kneels. SISSY gives him a strike of the belt.)

SISSY: Say you're sorry.

(BOY doesn't answer. SISSY strikes a second time, then a third and fourth during the following.)

SISSY: You think you know me. I know you make fun of me. You judge everyone, that's why no one likes you. That's why you didn't have friends at school. You always had to show everyone you were different. Well, everyone's different, every single person. We just don't show off about it.

(DAD wakes up.)

DAD: What's going on?

SISSY: He wasn't doing his exercises.

(DAD nods. SISSY strikes a fifth time.)

DAD: *(to SISSY)* Come here.

(SISSY approaches DAD. He takes the hat she's wearing. He examines it.)

SISSY: The rain. I didn't have an umbrella. I borrowed it.

DAD: A boy's hat.

SISSY: No.

(DAD strikes SISSY, a light swat.)

SISSY: A girl. Naomi. A girl.

DAD: I never heard that name.

SISSY: I swear to God.

DAD: You know what that means, swearing to God. *(SISSY nods.)* You swear to God you didn't get this from some boy. Some nice boy who just wanted to help out.

SISSY: No. I wouldn't. I wouldn't ever do that. Maybe it's her brother's hat.

DAD: She has a brother?

SISSY: I don't know, I never talked to her, it was just, raining, and she said she didn't want it.

DAD: How many was that?

SISSY: Three.

BOY SMALL: Six.

DAD: Probably enough. Make sure he finishes. *(Puts hat on SISSY's head and exits.)*

SISSY: *(shoves the burger into BOY's hand.)* Finish.

BOY SMALL: It's not that I don't want to. It just doesn't go down.

(SISSY exits, wearing her hat. BOY SMALL becomes BOY GROWN. He throws out the burger and returns to cage.)

BOY GROWN: It's like when they open the Big-Box right outside Crabtree. First the hardware store closes, but let's face it, the owner was kind of a prick. No matter how many times you go in asking for a metric screw, he'd never stock them. Couple weeks later, it's the pharmacy. Nice people, but six bucks for deodorant? After the fats break down, the proteins are next. Those long, amino acid chains of flower shops and bookstores and shoe stores that used to protect the vital organs, Town Hall and the library. But who needs those when you got overstock bins at the Big-Box?

Tom and Burt are holed up at the courthouse, trying to get it declared a historical landmark. They really think they can win money away from food stamps and Medicare. Don't they realize? Townsfolk need those to survive on their Big-Box paychecks. By Flag Day, Tom's made his own plaque. A nice piece of boxwood, engraved with the names and dates, and Burt nails it to the courthouse door. But no one who passes this way remembers how to read.

(He goes to sleep.)

(End of scene.)

SCENE 9: TEACHERS LOUNGE

(A few days later. TEACHER enters, a form in her hand. Her entrance defines a neutral space that represents a school hallway. She addresses us.)

TEACHER: Was notification to home school properly filed, please check yes or no. Yes? Or No? Let's see. First semester, I was his teacher. And right before winter break, he said he was going to live with his mommy. Which, he was always making up stories, so who knows. But come January, he didn't come back, and I missed him. He was a strange boy, but who isn't strange these days? They all think they're gonna be famous. But he listened. I missed that. Most of these kids don't even take the time to learn your name. But there's always one or two...

(SISSY passes, with backpack.)

SISSY: Hi, Miss Carmen.

TEACHER: Sissy! *(to us)* I had her two years ago. Nice girl. *(to SISSY)* What are you doing around these parts?

SISSY: Cutting through to get to gym.

TEACHER: You're still here?

SISSY: One more year.

TEACHER: Oh. So you didn't move.

SISSY: Move?

TEACHER: To your mom's. You guys moved, right? Or am I thinking of Terrence. He has a sister about your age.

SISSY: I don't think I know them.

TEACHER: They were here last semester. The dad had them, but then I think the aunt or somebody was taking them. God, these kids move around so much.

SISSY: School, I guess.

TEACHER: It's nice to see a familiar face. So only your brother moved. So it's *his* mom. So you're staying with *your* mom?

SISSY: He is being home schooled.

TEACHER: Huh?

SISSY: Sorry to cut through. I know we're not supposed to.

TEACHER: Sissy. Wait. He's being home schooled, just all of a sudden. What about you? Why aren't you being home schooled?

SISSY: Oh. I'm almost done.

TEACHER: Same school for six years. You're a walking record. Who's teaching him?

SISSY: My dad? Stepmom.

TEACHER: So you have a different mom. Like the Schmidt family. You know the Schmidts?

SISSY: I knew Kelsey.

TEACHER: They each had their own mom, but they were all in district. I knew all those kids by name.

SISSY: Just like me.

TEACHER: And a couple weeks later, notification form ends up on my desk. I don't know. He's a lucky kid. Parents who care enough to take all that time. *(to SISSY)* You get yourself to class. *(SISSY exits.)* A beautiful girl, but not like him. He's one of the special ones. Take some extra time with him and he could go anywhere. Notification received, yes or no? I guess. Yes.

(TEACHER checks off the form and exits.)

(End of scene.)

SCENE 10: NEW BEST FRIENDS

(A few days later. BOY sleeps in cage. SHERRY enters, carrying a juice box.)

SHERRY: *(calls behind her)* I said I was sorry!

BOY SMALL: *(drowsy)* What's going on? What happened?

(SHERRY opens the cage.)

SHERRY: Don't be nosy. Drink this.

BOY SMALL: I can't.

SHERRY: It's not food, okay? It's juice. Just a sip. Come on, you're freaking me out.

(BOY crawls out with some difficulty. SHERRY helps him sip from a juice box. He notices a mark on her face.)

BOY SMALL: What's that?

SHERRY: VISA bill came. Come on. A little more. *(Helps him.)* "Sissy's not out buying stuff." Yeah, 'cause you treat her like a two-year-old. What kid doesn't have a phone? What kid doesn't have at least lip gloss? I have to call every time I get to work, every time I get on break, but it's my fault when I'm out of minutes.

BOY SMALL: You're fun.

SHERRY: Fun.

BOY SMALL: You try stuff. You do stuff.

SHERRY: I'm a real inspiration.

BOY SMALL: You are.

SHERRY: *(pleased)* You're full of shit.

(SISSY enters hurriedly, backpack over her shoulder.)

SISSY: He's not here?

SHERRY: Beer run.

SISSY: I missed the bus. I ran. That's a cute top.

SHERRY: Want it?

SISSY: Huh? Do I…?

(SHERRY pulls off her top and throws it at SISSY.)

SHERRY: I'm sure it would look better on you. I need to get changed now. If you don't mind.

(SHERRY waits for SISSY to leave. SISSY is confused.)

SISSY: I've got his food.

BOY SMALL: Sherry already fed me.

SISSY: He ate? Does Daddy know? How did you…?

SHERRY: Guess I just have the touch.

SISSY: Sherry. If I did anything. If I said anything wrong.

SHERRY: You made me cut off the tags.

SISSY: Me? But, don't you remember—

SHERRY: Little Miss Innocent. You didn't do anything.

SISSY: I'll get them. I'll go in the garbage. I'll find them. I can tape them back on, no problem. Make them look brand new.

BOY SMALL: She's good at faking stuff.

SISSY: Shut up.

BOY SMALL: You shut up.

SHERRY: What does that mean.

SISSY: Nothing.

SHERRY: So go do it. If you'll allow me my privacy to dress.

(SISSY exits. SHERRY gets money from her purse.)

SHERRY: What do you mean, faking things? I'll give you a ten. A twenty.

BOY SMALL: *(changes subject)* You shouldn't listen to him. He did the same thing to Mommy. Except then he kept talking about his old girlfriend. How perfect she was.

SHERRY: You don't remember that.

BOY SMALL: I remember. When she cut her hair.

SHERRY: What is it with men and long hair.

BOY SMALL: It's not her fault. It's what he does. He makes you fake things.

SHERRY: He does.

BOY SMALL: You shouldn't.

SHERRY: No, you're right.

BOY SMALL: You should stand up for yourself.

SHERRY: Like you do. You don't fake things.

BOY SMALL: Sissy thinks she has to. Like when Mommy said the salon did it by mistake. Any idiot would know you're sitting there, you can stop them, right? But he believed her. Men and long hair.

SHERRY: He cares about dumb things. Like what time she gets home. She can't take five extra minutes? And what's in her backpack. What does he think would be in there?

BOY SMALL: And her hat. That stupid hat.

SHERRY: Who cares where she got it?

BOY SMALL: It's a boy's hat. Duh.

SHERRY: It's from a boy. Duh.

BOY SMALL: Dumb boy. Just like Dad.

SHERRY: You met him?

BOY SMALL: Kind of. More or less.

SHERRY: What's his name? Look at this, a nice twenty. Bet you don't have one of those.

(SHERRY gives BOY a twenty. He doesn't answer.)

SHERRY: Give you more for a name.

(BOY says nothing. SISSY returns. SHERRY shuts her purse.)

SISSY: The garbage men came. They're gone.

SHERRY: Doesn't matter. I'm good. *(to BOY)* You finish that juice. It's good for you.

SISSY: I'll make sure he finishes. Sherry. I'm sorry.

SHERRY: Tell your dad to wait up for me. I got a surprise for him.

SISSY: A surprise? Fun.

SHERRY: Hope so.

(SHERRY exits. SISSY hands BOY the juice box.)

SISSY: It's still full. You gotta have a little. You're supposed to do what I say. Or else.

(BOY crosses to bed and gets in position. Waits. SISSY gets a belt. She gets in position.)

BOY SMALL: Hurry up. My knees hurt.

SISSY: That's not my fault.

BOY SMALL: You're getting better at it. You're gonna be a real pro.

SISSY: Just shut up. You don't know anything about anything.

BOY SMALL: Then do it. You've been thinking about it all day. Every time you were too stupid to answer something in class. Ever think how weird it is that you're the one who gets to be in school?

(SISSY grabs the juice box.)

SISSY: Just give it to me.

(SISSY downs the rest of the juice.)

SISSY: There, you ate.

BOY SMALL: Maybe I wanted that, you pig.

SISSY: Brother boy, it was a brand new hat. Okay? He bought it for our first date. That's what he called it. Our first date. He wanted to have something new to wear. So there.

BOY SMALL: It was new.

SISSY: Not clean. Just new. I do listen to you. It stayed in my brain.

BOY SMALL: No.

SISSY: It's okay. Just forget it.

BOY SMALL: Sissy.

SISSY: It sort of brought us closer together. I didn't want to ask him, but I did. And then he told me. And then I was glad I did.

BOY SMALL: Sissy, I'm sorry.

SISSY: You should be. Now let's just forget it. Come on, get away from there.

BOY SMALL: No. Come on. Do it.

SISSY: Why?

BOY SMALL: I was mad at you.

SISSY: But now you're not.

BOY SMALL: Just come on. Once, even. For later.

SISSY: Why? What did you do?

BOY SMALL: I wasn't going to. I didn't mean to, exactly. I can say I made it up.

SISSY: Made what up?

BOY SMALL: About the hat.

SISSY: The hat.

BOY SMALL: Not him. Only her. She was upset. She needed something.

SISSY: So you gave her me.

BOY SMALL: You'll feel better. Come on. I don't mind. I want you to.

SISSY: You don't understand anything.

BOY SMALL: Maybe she'll forget. Maybe he'll be asleep when she gets home and she'll change her mind. I'll say I was mad at you, and I wanted the stupid hat, and so I made it up.

SISSY: I am stupid.

BOY SMALL: Don't say that. Only I get to say that.

DAD: *(offstage)* Sissy!

SISSY: I'm here! I thought I had time. Just a little time.

BOY SMALL: It's just a hat.

SISSY: Of course it's not just a hat. It's... *(She whacks her stomach with the belt.)*

BOY SMALL: What?

SISSY: You can't understand.

BOY SMALL: Isn't there a test?

SISSY: Of course. There's a million. But I had to buy one. And I had to do it at school...

(DAD enters, holding a six-pack. BOY is still kneeling at bed.)

DAD: Sherry left?

SISSY: *(still holding the belt.)* Uh-huh.

80

DAD: Look at you kids. You're teaching him, you're helping him. He eat?

BOY SMALL: A little.

DAD: Good boy.

BOY SMALL: I wouldn't eat, and then Sissy made me realize I should eat.

DAD: You know you reward the good behavior. That's important, too.

SISSY: Yes, Daddy.

DAD: *(to BOY)* One day, you keep getting better, we sit back, have a beer, we know what we came through. It's earned.

BOY SMALL: Earned, yes.

DAD: My little girl. You got him to eat. *(Hugs SISSY, a little too long.)* You my good girl?

SISSY: Yes, Daddy.

DAD: Want my wife. Want my phone. Want sleep.

SISSY: You're tired, Daddy. *(Eases out of the hug and helps DAD onto the bed.)*

DAD: You know me.

SISSY: I got it. I think he'll eat a little more.

DAD: Let him… stay out a little…

(DAD passes out. SISSY and BOY whisper, away from DAD.)

BOY SMALL: *(quietly)* So you might be.

SISSY: *(quietly)* I did it at lunch. You have to pee on it. And then it started… but the bell rang. I think I saw it start to make a cross, but then the hall monitor came in—

BOY SMALL: You had the whole lunch period. Why would you wait 'til the end?

SISSY: I was hungry.

BOY SMALL: Sissy. You gotta get away from here.

SISSY: Mommy had me young.

BOY SMALL: You cannot tell her. You cannot go there.

SISSY: I want her.

BOY SMALL: She will call him. No. *(Digs out his stash of money.)* Sissy, you have to go somewhere he can never find you. Use this.

SISSY: What?

BOY SMALL: What do you think I been saving for.

SISSY: Your next chance.

BOY SMALL: This is it.

SISSY: He'll change his mind. He always does.

BOY SMALL: And when he finds out?

SISSY: Brother boy. Please don't let him. I'll do something.

BOY SMALL: You'll go.

SISSY: Not by myself. I can't.

BOY SMALL: Yes you can.

SISSY: No I can't.

BOY SMALL: Yes you can.

DAD: *(rouses)* You kids. Call Sherry. Tell her come straight home. I want my family. A family night.

SISSY: Make her leave work?

DAD: Sure. Fuck them.

SISSY: Look, Daddy, he ate it all. He's going to do his homework.

DAD: Good boy. Want my family. It's what I work for.

SISSY: You work hard. Want another beer?

DAD: Mm. Take a piss.

(DAD exits.)

BOY SMALL: Now take it.

SISSY: *(takes the money)* What do I. Where do I…

BOY SMALL: What about Brendan-Ethan? What about this grandma of his.

SISSY: She's gone back home.

BOY SMALL: Where's home? Don't tell me where. That's where you have to go.

SISSY: It's far.

BOY SMALL: Good.

SISSY: But he'll hurt Brendan-Ethan.

BOY SMALL: I didn't tell his name. I didn't want her to think I was making it up.

SISSY: I like his name.

BOY SMALL: Does he know?

SISSY: We talked about it kind of. I said, if I was. And he said, if I was, then. And then we didn't talk about it anymore.

BOY SMALL: You're gonna need more.

(BOY approaches DAD's wallet.)

SISSY: Please don't.

(DAD enters with two beers. He hands one to BOY.)

DAD: Celebrate. You finally shaping up. Good meal. And a drink.

BOY SMALL: Beer?

DAD: It's earned. To me.

(They toast. BOY sips, then coughs his up.)

DAD: Good, that means you haven't been sneaking 'em.

(They continue to drink, BOY doing everything to keep his small sips down.)

DAD: She tries to hide that bill. Every month. Like I don't know what day it is. Like I don't know her. Doesn't think. They don't want to think. You're different, Sissy.

SISSY: Yes.

DAD: Yeah?

SISSY: Yeah.

(BOY edges over to the wallet.)

DAD: She thinks I don't know what she's doing. But that tells me exactly what she's doing.

BOY SMALL: It's not right.

DAD: Toast that.

(DAD and BOY toast.)

BOY SMALL: End of the month is hard.

DAD: Tell me about it. Another bill from the paper. I said I don't even want it. They said okay, they'll stop sending it. No they don't stop sending it. They send overdue bill. What the fuck?

(BOY has money from DAD's wallet, sneaks back to cage.)

BOY SMALL: Sissy could call them.

DAD: Yeah. Call them. I wanna talk to them. Don't they know we're human? We're trying to have a life here. Trying to get out from under. On top of that, Jesus, I can't even talk about it.

SISSY: Not if it upsets you, Daddy.

DAD: Fucking, where I live, right in the, in between where the living is.

BOY SMALL: You go call the paper, Sis.

(BOY forces money into SISSY's hand.)

SISSY: No.

DAD: Eight hundred number. Bring me the phone.

SISSY: But I don't...

BOY SMALL: Go.

(BOY and SISSY hug goodbye. SISSY exits.)

DAD: Tell me something. Tell me your homework.

BOY SMALL: I don't do homework anymore.

DAD: *(falling asleep)* Mm. Tell me.

(BOY tries to return to cage but is too weak, becomes BOY GROWN.)

BOY GROWN: Clichés are made, not born. I learned that. Neurons travelling the same paths over and over. People get what they deserve, because of these pathways. People know what they feel, 'cause of them.

(Lights shift. SHERRY enters in a slipdress, barefoot; slips into bed with DAD.)

BOY GROWN: A beautiful woman is beautiful because she aligns with the longings burned into our pathways. It's good to remember, beauty comes to she who burns long enough.

(DAD wakes a little; they kiss. BOY GROWN becomes BOY SMALL.)

DAD: *(to SHERRY)* Come straight home?

SHERRY: Of course.

DAD: You didn't call.

SHERRY: I couldn't. Anyway you were sleeping.

DAD: Not sleeping. Talking to my kids.

SHERRY: Talking?

DAD: Talking. This family thing.

SHERRY: She told you?

DAD: Told me. What did she tell me.

SHERRY: Or did he. He's the one who told me.

DAD: *(fully awake now)* Told what.

SHERRY: About the boyfriend.

DAD: *(shoves SHERRY)* And you didn't tell me? Sissy. Get in here!

SHERRY: She deserves what she gets. I didn't tell. I wasn't going to tell. It's not my fault.

(BOY doesn't answer. DAD returns.)

DAD: Where the fuck is she.

SHERRY: She's not here?

BOY SMALL: Gone.

(DAD puts on belt and shoes.)

DAD: Gone. *(to SHERRY)* Get my keys. Call her mother. That's where she'll be. Then I'll find this kid. Who is he? Where does he live?

SHERRY: *(points to BOY)* He knows. He does.

DAD: *(to BOY)* Tell me. *(BOY tries to crawl to cage.)* You don't get away from me. *(DAD pulls BOY toward him.)*

BOY SMALL: I did. Me and Sissy, we both got away.

SHERRY: What's he saying.

DAD: You tell me what you know.

BOY SMALL: Yes, sir. His name is… Let's see. He lives… Oh yes, he lives, right, exactly, somewhere. Or was it nowhere. Oh that's right, it was anywhere.

DAD: *(shaking him)* Don't play with me.

BOY SMALL: I was wrong. You have to win. Always. That's why you lose.

(DAD strikes BOY.)

SHERRY: Please.

(DAD grabs SHERRY's phone.)

DAD: Let me talk to her mom. Hello?

SHERRY: I couldn't. I'm out of minutes.

DAD: *(throws SHERRY's phone)* You both knew. Both in on it.

SHERRY: No. I just found out. I swear.

DAD: Get in the car.

SHERRY: What about him?

(DAD tries to get BOY into the cage.)

DAD: Get up. Go on, get in there. *(BOY doesn't move.)* 'Deal with him later.

(DAD and SHERRY exit.

BOY tries to move; can't. He rests a little.)

BOY SMALL: Don't be there, Sissy. Please don't be at Mommy's. Anywhere but there.

SISSY: *(entering)* I'm here!

BOY SMALL: You're gone.

SISSY: I snuck back. I had to. I wanted to. Here. *(Gives him the hat.)* Only got it for you in the first place.

BOY SMALL: Smells like you now.

SISSY: Gross.

BOY SMALL: Did you hear something?

SISSY: Is that them?

(They listen.)

BOY SMALL: You have to go. They're looking for you.

SISSY: You're sure you'll be okay? Maybe I shouldn't. I don't have to. But you'll be okay? Brother boy?

BOY SMALL: Sissy.

SISSY: Okay. I should. I better. Okay.

(SISSY exits. BOY SMALL becomes BOY GROWN, gets up.)

BOY GROWN: I'm not dead when they come back. But I never get up again. It takes another twelve hours for my heart to stop. Then he takes a whole day figuring out what to do. Poor guy can't even bury me right.

Doesn't go far enough. Doesn't dig deep enough. Uses the cheapest quick-drying cement. Might as well hang a sign. He puts a Bible on my chest, like an offering to the cops, the only Gods he knows. Still, it takes them two years to find me. And by then, Sissy is far away. People are busy in this world. You can't see everything all at once. If you could you'd be blind. That's why I'm here, still here, through all this time. We do the best we can, at the time, but she won't remember that. I don't think of it until she's gone, that she will need forgiveness. Or that I had it to give. And now it's too late. But like I told you, I'm selfish in my suffering. Truly, I recognize no one's but my own.

(BOY puts on hat and exits.)

(End of play.)

More Great Plays From Original Works Publishing

Nurture by Johnna Adams

Synopsis: Doug and Cheryl are horrible single parents drawn together by their equally horrible daughters. The star-crossed parental units' journey from first meeting to first date, to first time, to first joint parent-teacher meeting, to proposal and more. They attempt to form a modern nuclear family while living in perpetual fear of the fruit of their loins and someone abducting young girls in their town.

Cast Size: 1 Male, 1 Female

Harry and the Thief by Sigrid Gilmer

Synopsis: Mimi's cousin Jeremy has a PhD in physics, a brand new time machine and a plan. He's sending Mimi, a professional thief, back to 1863 to change history by providing Harriet Tubman with modern day guns. Lots and lots of guns.

Cast Size: Diverse Cast of 10 Actors

American Girls by Hilary Bettis

Synopsis: In a celebrity driven culture, BFF's Katie and Amanda are at a cross-roads. They are two God fearing Iowa girls fresh out of middle school, but have their sights set on much bigger things. They want fame, even if it means selling their souls to the Devil in the name of the Bible. If they can achieve their goals the boys will croon with lust and the mean girls will cry with envy. Pastor Jim preaches the Lords way while the girls pursue their Hollywood dreams in the big city. Flush with naivete the girls journey takes them down a dark and seedy path, putting them at odds with one another and forcing them to grow up much too fast.

Cast Size: 1 Male, 2 Females, (1 Female on video)

Virus Attacks Heart by Shannon Murdoch
Synopsis: Beatrice is trying for a less crazy life but her walls are talking to her and she can't stay home any longer. Jamie has just stepped off a train in a new city and is searching for something to make him new again. One spilled drink in a dingy nightclub with bad music propels these two characters into a night of sex, alcohol and stories as they push and pull and test each others limits as they search for a connection that goes deeper than flesh. Unfolding in a non-linear structure, Virus Attacks Heart is an intricate, poetic dissection of one night in two strangers lives.
Cast Size: 1 Male, 1 Female

NOTES

NOTES

NOTES

NOTES

Made in the USA
Middletown, DE
07 April 2016